This book belongs to:

____

24 23 22 21 1 2 3 4

Published by Tughra Books
335 Clifton Ave.
Clifton, NJ, 07011, USA
www.tughrabooks.com

ISBN 979-8-89729-505-0

Mini Muslims Series ISBN 9781597849692

WHAT ARE Angels?

Allah created Angels.

They are made of light, have wings,

and glorify Allah.

They do whatever Allah tells them to do and they never disobey Him.

They pray, worship, and serve Allah

all the time.

There are special Angels
that are given jobs by Allah.

Angel Jibreel revealed the Quran
to Prophet Muhammad (pbuh).

There are also many more!

We believe in
all **the Angels**!